THE EXPLANAT
of
JUDE & 2 PET]

CW01497328

by
BLESSED THEOPHYLACT
Archbishop of Ochrid and Bulgaria

This volume is part of the series:
BLESSED THEOPHYLACT'S EXPLANATIONS

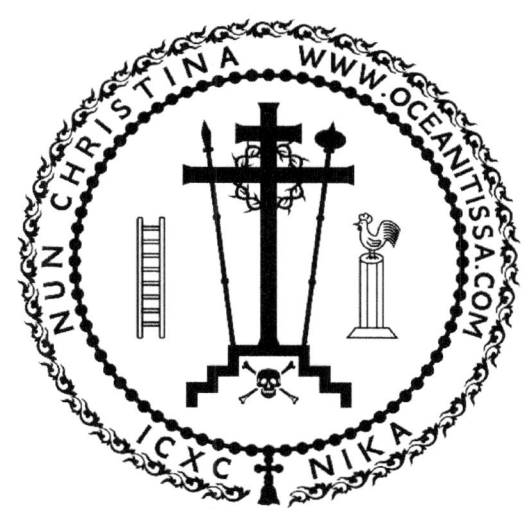

Nun Christina
Anna Skoubourdis

Published by: Virgin Mary of Australia and Oceania 2023 ©
oceanitissa@gmail.com
www.oceanitissa.com.au
Youtube: Nun Christina Oceanitissa

The Explanation of 2 Peter

Summary

This second epistle, like the first, is also addressed by Peter to those who have already come to faith; the epistle is a reminder of what he had said before. For he knows that his body will soon be *put off*, and so he is diligent to remind everyone of the teaching that they had initially received. First, he expounds the faith, showing that it had been proclaimed as gospel beforehand by the prophets, and that the prophecies about the Savior are not from men, but were spoken from God. Next, he urges them to pay no heed to the *deceivers*, saying that their destruction will come, just as it had for *the angels that sinned*. He foretells in the epistle that days will come in which *scoffers will walk about* and desire to deceive some, saying that all our talk of the Savior's coming is but idle chatter, for it is always spoken of, but has not yet come to pass. Peter instructs them to avoid such men in particular, and explains how God is not unaware of the time; all time is nothing before the Lord, *for one day is like a thousand years, and a thousand years is like one day*. Peter reassures them and shows that the day of the Lord will come quickly. He enjoins them all to be ready with good works, and to love the writings of the Apostle Paul, paying no attention to those who speak ill of them, for they speak ill of all the holy Scriptures. So having reminded them and taught them all *to know these things before*, he exhorts them not to *fall short* of the goal of their faith. And that is how he concludes the letter.[1]

---

[1] All Scripture references and versification follow the King James Version (KJV), except where the original wording is of particular relevance to Theophylact's argument. In such cases, the Greek is rendered more directly, and the KJV text is given in a footnote.

Major Themes

i.   *On the calling in faith that is confirmed by works of virtue, and hope of good things to come.*

ii.   *Exhortation to remember his teaching after he is gone; and how he heard the voice of God speaking of Christ on Mount Tabor.*

iii.   *Foretelling the rise of heretical deceivers, and the coming punishment of their ungodliness.*

iv.   *Repetition of the evil of heretical men.*

a.   *Christ will come suddenly at the consummation of this age.*

b.   *Thus, one must avail oneself of every virtue.*

Chapter 1

1:1-2. Simeon Peter,[2] also an apostle of Jesus Christ, to them that have obtained like precious faith with us through the righteousness of God and our Saviour Jesus Christ. Grace and peace be multiplied unto you through the knowledge of God, and of Jesus our Lord [...] "Simeon" or "Simon" for short, just like "Metras" is short for "Metrodoros", "Menas" is short for "Menodoros", and "Theudas" is short for "Theodosios". From the very opening of the letter, he excites the thoughts and souls of the believers, elevating them to the same zeal for preaching the gospel that the apostles have. For he says, "It is not right for those *who have obtained like precious faith* to fall short of their equals in any regard." Everywhere he seeks to motivate them through *peace*, the same *peace* that Christ gave when he was resurrected from the dead and went to the Father, calling out: *Peace be unto you.*[3] We also pray for "an angel of peace" to be given to the church. Likewise, the priest also offers *peace* to the people from the holy altar, for *peace* is the mother of all good things. That is why the Lord commanded his disciples to bestow it as the first gift when entering a house.[4] This is the logical sequence: "To you who have obtained like precious faith with us in the knowledge of our God and of Christ Jesus our Lord, through the righteousness of our God, grace and peace be multiplied."

1:3-4a. According as his divine power hath given unto us all things that pertain unto life and godliness, through the knowledge of him that hath called us to glory and virtue: Whereby are given unto us exceeding great and precious promises [...] This is the logical sequence: "Grace to you and peace, as well as all things that pertain unto life and godliness through the knowledge of God and Jesus our Lord, whose grace has been given to us by his divine power unto the knowledge of glory and virtue, whereby are given unto us exceeding great promises; that by these ye might be partakers of the divine nature, having escaped the corruption that is in the world through lust." *Otherwise.* The meaning of this long digression is this: "Because we have received countless blessings by the power of Christ, we can become partakers of the divine nature, and advance in life and godliness,

---

[2] KJV: *Simon Peter, a servant and an apostle.* Textual variant.
[3] John 20:19.
[4] Luke 10:5.

so we should conduct ourselves accordingly, to add to our faith virtue, and progress through virtue according to godliness, until we reach the perfection of all good things, which is love." We have become partakers of the divine nature through the incarnation of the Lord our God, who took unto himself the first fruits of our nature and sanctified what he had taken; *and if the firstfruit be holy, the lump is also holy.*[5] Peter calls what is in the world through lust *corruption*, because it is formed out of perishing things and concerns itself with them.

1:4b. [...] that by these ye might be partakers of the divine nature, having escaped the corruption that is in the world through lust. This is the logical sequence: "That, having been freed from the corruption that is in the world, which is in fleshly lust, you might become partakers of the divine nature." For, *having escaped* means "having been freed from".

1:5-7. And beside this, giving all diligence, add to your faith virtue; and to virtue knowledge; and to knowledge temperance; and to temperance patience; and to patience godliness; and to godliness brotherly kindness; and to brotherly kindness charity. Peter comprehends levels of progress: the first is *faith*, which is the foundation and basis of all good things. The second is *virtue*, or "works", for without them faith is *dead*, as James says.[6] After them comes *knowledge*. What is this? "The comprehension of the hidden mysteries of God", which does not delight to dwell in just anyone, but only in him who has accustomed himself to good works through training. Next comes *temperance*. For he who has attained his goal in some measure also has need of this, lest he grow haughty at the *greatness* of what he *has been given*. He who makes but small use of *temperance* cannot take firm hold of what he *has been given*, for the passions always tend to exacerbate the things that stifle his freedom. Then *patience* comes in and finishes the task, giving rise to *godliness*, and rendering trust in God more complete. And thus *brotherly kindness* is added to *godliness*, and *charity*, the fulfillment of all good things, is added above all, as Paul rightly says. For this is what compelled both the Son of God and

---

[5] Romans 11:16.
[6] James 2:17.

his Father: the Father to give his beloved Son, and the Son to shed his blood on our behalf.

1:8. For if these things be in you, and abound, they make you that ye shall neither be barren nor unfruitful in the knowledge of our Lord Jesus Christ. *These things.* What things? *Faith, virtue, knowledge, temperance, patience, godliness, brotherly kindness, charity.* These must not only be present, but *abound.* For if their very presence is of benefit, how much more their proliferation! And what other benefit do they confer than that one might have confidence at the second coming of the Lord? For the one who does not have these things in him will certainly go *blind* when the Judge appears in glory, shining like the sun; even if his eyesight be strong, not even then could he gaze unharmed upon the surpassing radiance of him whose nature gives off eternal light to blind the eyes of those who look upon him in their frailty.

1:9-10a. But he that lacketh these things is blind, and cannot see afar off, and hath forgotten that he was purged from his old sins. Wherefore the rather, brethren, give diligence to make your calling and election sure [...] The phrase *cannot see afar off* in Greek refers to the utter blindness of moles that live underground. This is like what the Blessed James says: *For if any be a hearer of the word, and not a doer, he is like unto a man beholding his natural face in a glass.*[7] And once he has beheld himself through the purification of holy baptism, being washed clean of a multitude of sins, he must realize that he received holiness when he was purified, and he must be soberminded in order to maintain that holiness, *without which no one will see the Lord.*[8] But he has forgotten this. *Wherefore the rather, brethren, give diligence to make your calling and election sure.* That means "be blameless" in your *calling* and the teaching you received when you were *elected*, that you might not be judged as having forgotten what *you were given* by God, but rather remain, being *sure of your calling.*

1:10b-12a. [...] for if ye do these things, ye shall never fall: for so an entrance shall be ministered unto you abundantly into the everlasting

---

[7] James 1:23.
[8] Hebrews 12:14.

kingdom of our Lord and Saviour Jesus Christ. Wherefore I will not be negligent to put you always in remembrance of these things [...] *For if ye do these things.* Which things? Those that he has just enumerated: *virtue, knowledge*, and so on. Notice how first he argued from the terrors of the judgment seat, while now he argues from the blessings of the *entrance into the everlasting kingdom* of God.

1:12b-14. [...] though ye know them, and be established in the present truth. Yea, I think it meet, as long as I am in this tabernacle, to stir you up by putting you in remembrance; Knowing that shortly I must put off this my tabernacle, even as our Lord Jesus Christ hath shewed me. Lest his hearers be discouraged and think that he is condemning them for laziness by constantly reminding them about the same things, Peter says, *though ye know them, and be established in the present truth.* He further gives the reason for his frequent reminders: he knows that he will be leaving this body *shortly.*

1:15. Moreover I will endeavour that ye may be able after my decease to have these things always in remembrance. Some rearrange the order of the sentence to say, "I will endeavor also after my decease to have you in remembrance of these things always" (that is, "every day" and "continually"). They wish to prove by this that even after their death the saints remember us here, and they intercede on behalf of the living, for they observe that those who call on their divine grace day by day are not without manifest faith. Others interpret the passage more simply to mean, "I will endeavor that you may be able after my decease to have these things always in remembrance." That is, "This is the reason why I continually persist in imploring you, not to condemn you for not listening or understanding, but rather that I might accustom you to these things and that you might take hold of them firmly and solidly and have certain and indelible instructions concerning them, even after I have died."

1:16. For we have not followed cunningly devised fables, when we made known unto you the power and coming of our Lord Jesus Christ, but were eyewitnesses of his majesty. Peter has said how they should apply themselves diligently to the gospel that he is presenting and has spoken at length about it, even though they already know it and have heard various accounts of it. He now goes on to say: "It is not for no reason that am so meticulous about these things, but rather I insist on them because I know how crucial they are." How crucial what is? *"To make known unto you the power and coming of our Lord*, and not to use human wisdom on you and enchant your ears with sweet-sounding words. For that is what the Greeks and the heretics do. The Greeks deceive by adorning their words with poetry, and the heretics by their artifice (heresies would have already started to spring up by this time). Therefore nothing of the sort is to be found in us. We have cast our teaching to you in plain words, just as Paul said to the Corinthians,[9] including what we saw with our own eyes, those of us who went up with him to the *holy mount*." He is speaking of *the glory [...] of the only begotten*,[10] which he showed them in the transfiguration, and the voice of the Father which they heard *coming from heaven* on behalf of the Lord.[11] "And since we apprehended through the events what the prophets had proclaimed beforehand, we can now judge the prophecy to be *more sure* because of it. For the events have followed after the words. So you also *do well that ye take heed of the prophecy*, that is, 'what was spoken by the prophets beforehand', even if it was only hinted at darkly by the prophets back then."

1:17a. For having received[12] from God the Father honour and glory [...]
The participial form *having received* either means the same as the finite verb "he received" since the rest of the sentence does not offer a finite verb for the participle to refer to, which is required by the rules of syntax; or else, if one should insist on taking *having received* as a bona fide participle, the sentence must necessarily descend into grammatical disarray. But if we take the participle *having received* as a finite verb "he received", then the logical sense would be: *For he received from God the Father honour and glory.*

1:17b-19. [...] when there came such a voice to him from the excellent glory, This is my beloved Son, in whom I am well pleased. And this voice which came from heaven we heard, when we were with him in the

---

[9] 1 Corinthians 2:4.
[10] John 1:14.
[11] Matthew 17:5.
[12] KJV: *he received.* The KJV, like Theophylact, compensates for the lack of a main verb in this clause.

holy mount. We have also a more sure word of prophecy; whereunto ye do well that ye take heed, as unto a light that shineth in a dark place, until the day dawn, and the day star arise in your hearts. Not that there is any prophecy about the voice that came from the Father on high, but rather because of the voice that came from the Father on high testifying that Jesus is his Son, we have sure grounds to apply every oracle spoken through the prophets unerringly to the one to whom the Father has born witness. We know of three times that the Father bore witness that our Lord Jesus Christ is his Son: at his baptism,[13] during his passion (when he said, *I have both glorified [your name], and will glorify it again*),[14] and *in the mount*. Peter says, "If you *take heed* of what the prophets said, you will not fail to achieve your hope. For the events will come to pass according to their own time (which he calls *day* in keeping with the metaphor, since he had already mentioned a *light* and a *dark place*, where it is night). So when the *day* comes, by which I mean, 'when the events comes to pass', you will have *the day star arise in your hearts*, that is the coming of Christ, foretold by the prophets, and illuminating your heats as the true *light*."

1:20-21. Knowing this first, that no prophecy of the scripture is of his own[15] interpretation. For the prophecy came not in old time by the will of man: but holy men of God spake as they were moved by the Holy Ghost. The prophets knew both what the Spirit of prophecy was inspiring them with and what they were speaking of; however, they did not know exactly how everything would be carried out. And so they desired to see the how it would be implemented in detail, as the Lord says.[16] Peter goes on to explain why the prophets did not interpret what they said, and at the same time he distinguishes true prophecy from demonic and false prophecy, which can also be found among the heretics. *No prophecy of the scripture is of his own interpretation*. That means that while the prophets received the prophecy from God, they did not receive it according to their will, but as the Spirit of God impelled them. They both knew and understood the prophetic speech that was being sent down to them, and yet they gave no

---

[13] Matthew 3:17.

[14] John 12:28.

[15] KJV: *any private*. The KJV interprets "his own" as "anyone's own", while Theophylact takes it as "the prophet's own".

[16] Luke 10:24.

interpretation for it. The prophets who were impelled by the Spirit of God were aware that the word that was being sent down to them was from the Spirit of God. This is clear from the fact that they served willingly and only said what they wished to say, not saying anything they did not wish to say. That is not the way of the false prophets. For they did not remain aware when they are under impulsion, but rather they were moved erratically by a wild frenzy, not knowing what they are doing, like drunken men. While the holy prophets on the other hand kept their awareness, but did not need to interpret what they said; for they were serving others with their words (that is—us), and at the same time ensuring that the coming of the Lord remained a mystery, lest it be sabotaged by the ungodly. Not that it could not have been accomplished by the Lord's power even if they had sabotaged it. But since this was avoided on occasion by mysterious prophecies, it only made the undertaking of the incarnation seem all the more miraculous. The truth of this claim is clearly demonstrated by many, if not all, of the prophets of the New Testament, who interpreted their own prophecies as they gave them; for there was no need for this kind of subterfuge in the New Testament. It is moreover evident that these prophets did not deliver their oracles in a state of maniacal frenzy. For the prophets of both the Old and the New Testament prophesy out of one Spirit, as Paul says: *If any thing be revealed to another that sitteth by, let the first hold his peace.*[17] This clearly means that the prophets would stand up in their right minds and prophesy of their own accord. And so when another was inspired to stand up, the first was commanded to stop speaking and *hold his peace*, which no one would expect of a frenzied madman. For how can one *hold his peace* if he does not even know what he is doing? As Paul himself says, it is the Holy Spirit who works in the prophets: *For to one is given by the Spirit the word of wisdom; to another the word of knowledge by the same Spirit.*[18]

---

[17] 1 Corinthians 14:30.
[18] 1 Corinthians 12:8.

Chapter 2

2:1-3a. But there were false prophets also among the people, even as there shall be false teachers among you, who privily shall bring in damnable heresies, even denying the Lord that bought them, and bring upon themselves swift destruction. And many shall follow their pernicious ways; by reason of whom the way of truth shall be evil spoken of. And through covetousness shall they with feigned words make merchandise of you [...] *False prophets* refers to the followers of Nicolaus and Cerinthus. Peter wants to ensure that they do not listen to false prophets, since both prophets and false prophets alike bear the name of "prophecy". Paul teaches how to tell them apart: *no man can say that Jesus is the Lord, but by the Holy Ghost.*[19] Here begins Peter's invective against the Nicolaitan heresy. Their wickedness is twofold: their doctrine is blatantly irreverent, which is shown by their blasphemy against Christ the Lord, and their lives are *pernicious*. This he now proceeds to demonstrate from their wicked behavior, giving a clear example in the next verse: *covetousness*, which refers to "ill-gotten gain". *Covetousness* can sometimes mean "unrighteousness", and sometimes simply "ill-gotten gain". And so he naturally says that they *make merchandise of you* as well. According to Peter, they are far removed from the teaching of God and use *feigned words*. But he assures us that they will have the reward of their *pernicious ways*—death.

2:3b. [...] whose judgment now of a long time lingereth not, and their damnation slumbereth not. *Now of a long time* refers to the foreknowledge of God. Just as he in his providence has prepared good things for good people, so also he has prepared an appropriate place for evil people.

2:4-9. For if God spared not the angels that sinned, but cast them down to hell, and delivered them into chains of darkness, to be reserved unto judgment; and spared not the old world, but saved Noah the eighth person, a preacher of righteousness, bringing in the flood upon the world of the ungodly; and turning the cities of Sodom and Gomorrha into ashes condemned them with an overthrow, making them an

---

[19] 1 Corinthians 12:3.

ensample unto those that after should live ungodly; and delivered just Lot, vexed with the filthy conversation of the wicked: (for that righteous man dwelling among them, in seeing and hearing, vexed his righteous soul from day to day with their unlawful deeds). The Lord knoweth how to deliver the godly out of temptations, and to reserve the unjust unto the day of judgment to be punished. Peter is not simply making an argument from the greater to the lesser, but he also wishes to show that these apostates fall under even greater condemnation for their sin. Because of their privileged position (for they were the first to be called to apostleship), once they *forsook the right way*, they likewise incurred harsher judgment. Since Peter is merely using this example to buttress his argument, he does not give the conclusion to his hypothetical statement, but rather mixes into the example the idea of righteous men being saved. He ought to complete the thought that he began at first concerning those who had sinned, which is why he gave the example in the first place, and say something like: "If he did not spare them, then will he really spare those ungodly men who live now?" or to cast it as an assertion, "Then how much less will he spare them!" But Peter does not do this. Why? Because he has now given two examples, one positive and one negative, and this statement only answers to the negative example, and does not apply to the positive; for good men are not rewarded with evil. So the reason why the phrasing is different is because Peter was not content to conclude the passage with a single statement, but rather added on a final coda to complete the thought. But why does he include the examples of good men among the negative examples at all? We will answer this more fully in its appropriate place, but for now we will say that the logic of the passage does not follow the visible structure of the text. For we do not find the conclusion that would normally follow such constructions. Rather, the examples are purely to prove a point, that some are punished for sin, and others are honored for righteousness. It is as if Peter had said, "God knows how to punish those who live in their sins without clemency or relenting, like *the angels that sinned*, the generation of the flood, or the cities of Sodom. And, on the other hand, he knows how to honor those who practice righteousness, like Noah and Lot." This is the logical sequence. Having said that the false teachers would be punished for their blasphemies and their *pernicious ways*, he gives the examples: *For God did not spare the angels that sinned [...] nor the old world*. And he goes on to explain that those who practiced righteousness like Noah and Lot were saved because of their temperance from the destruction that came upon their generation. For Noah was not led away by the irreverence of the generation before the flood. And Lot was not enamored of the ungodliness of the Sodomites, but even refused to deliver over the angels who had lodged with him in the form of men to those who were demanding them for their wicked purposes; and that even though they heaped derision on him. This is the implication of *vexed*. And Peter goes on to say this about Lot as well: *The Lord knoweth how to deliver the godly out of temptations*, etc. Even though Peter had not said anything about just men up to this point, but only about ungodly men and their punishment, he still includes these examples. First, this is because the story mentions both the destruction of the ungodly and the salvation of the just at the same time. And secondly to juxtapose the two, throwing the evil of the sinners into relief, and the good works of the just. And finally to convince his listeners to eschew ungodliness because of punishment, and to be drawn to do good works on account of salvation.

2:10. But chiefly them that walk after the flesh in the lust of uncleanness, and despise dominion.[20] Presumptuous [are they], selfwilled, they are not afraid to speak evil of dignities. Here, Peter masterfully transitions from the previous examples back to the matter at hand. He is speaking of the accursed Nicolaitans, Naasenes, and Cerdonians. For their evil goes by many names, and its nomenclature is as confused as its vile practices. As we were saying, they posit *bythos* and *sigē* as the authors that brought the world into being, and invent fables of the *mētērs* and *aeons* which proceeded from them, just as Marcion did, having taken the seeds of his evil from them. Thus, they reject the idea that *dominion*, or "the Lord", created and maintains the world, and they proceed without fear to every kind of fleshly defilement. If anyone wishes to learn more about this, let him take to hand the exhaustive book written by Irenaeus the Celt concerning them, called, *Against Heresies*. A certain Marcus, a depraved reprobate, will be found to have perpetrated most of these sins, and defiled the women who followed him. The others also committed further atrocities, which cannot even be put in writing, for the very mention of them is defiling. For those who had no respect, but rather *despised dominion*, what matter would it be for them to lose all respect for any *dignity* whatsoever?

---

[20] KJV: *government*. Theophylact interprets this word as a reference to the Lord.

The blessed Apostle Jude is even more explicit about this, when he speaks of the body of Moses.[21] Peter, on the other hand, only touches on the subject here, and no sooner has he mentioned it, than he resumes his discourse. So we will follow his lead and continue on: *Presumptuous, selfwilled, they are not afraid to speak evil of dignities.* One must mentally supply the words "are they". *Unafraid of dignities* means, "they behave impudently and are not afraid to blaspheme any dignity."

2:11. Whereas angels, which are greater in power and might, bring not railing accusation against them before the Lord. Peter wants them to refrain from presumption in these matters, saying: *Whereas angels, which are greater in power and might, bring not railing accusation against them before the Lord.* As we have already mentioned, this is exactly what the Blessed Jude also says; for he likewise censures the endless babbling of certain people, crafting his admonishment out of the same example. Jude, however, goes into more depth: *Yet Michael the archangel [...] durst not bring against him a railing accusation.*[22] Something like this is what Peter is saying here as well: "These good-for-nothings have no inhibitions about speaking evil of dignities, while even those who are greater in power and might ("greater", that is, "than these vile men") bring not railing accusation against them before the Lord, that is, 'they do not slander the dignities'. For even the devil has some measure of *dignity*, since he was the first of the Lord's creations, and so Michael did not utter a slanderous word against him. So if Michael did not bring *railing accusation before the Lord* against the one who most deserves it (that is, "the devil") since he has a measure of *dignity*, then it must be the height of impudence when these men lightly *speak evil of dignities*, for they are far below the angels in honor. *Dignities* refers to the powers of God, or the authorities in the church, whom these men were opposing by *speaking evil* of them.

2:12-13a. But these, as natural brute beasts, made to be taken and destroyed, speak evil of the things that they understand not; and shall utterly perish in their own corruption; and shall receive the reward of unrighteousness, as they that count it pleasure to riot in the day time

---

[21] Jude 9.
[22] Jude 9.

[...] Some explain the passage this way: *They shall utterly perish in their own corruption, as natural brute beasts*, that is, "they are no better than animals, born only to perish." *As natural brute beasts* means "living only for sensual pleasures, not a life of thought and contemplation". This is why they are easily *taken* by the cares of this life, which is doomed to *corruption*, and are led about and controlled by anger and desire. *Of the things that they understand not*, that is, "they speak evil in their natural state of ignorance and will perish in the corruption that befits them." *And they shall receive the reward of unrighteousness*, which they have brought on themselves by their own free will. *As they that count it pleasure to riot in the day time*, meaning that they consider the enjoyment they get from satisfying their stomach every day to be their ultimate goal, true joy, and worthwhile happiness. Now, consider that when holy Scripture wishes to censure any of the natural instincts of people at the animal level, it compares them to brute beasts. *Nevertheless man being in honour abideth not: he is like the beasts that perish.*[23] *Be ye not as the horse, or as the mule.*[24] *They were as fed horses in the morning: every one neighed after his neighbour's wife.*[25] *Be ye therefore wise as serpents, and harmless as doves.*[26] It does not say this to change our natures, but simply calls us to refrain from the natural impulses for these things. And when it commends something that pertains to salvation, it draws more exalted analogies, such as: *Be ye therefore merciful, as your Father also is merciful.*[27] It is not trying to change our natures here either, but instructing us to do as much as is in our power.

2:13b-16. Spots they are and blemishes, well trained in avarice[28] while they feast with you; having eyes full of adultery, and that cannot cease from sin; beguiling unstable souls: an heart they have exercised with covetous practices; cursed children: which have forsaken the right way, and are gone astray, following the way of Balaam the son of Bosor, who loved the wages of unrighteousness; but was rebuked for his iniquity: the dumb ass speaking with man's voice forbad the madness of the

---

[23] Psalm 49:12.

[24] Psalm 32:9.

[25] Jeremiah 5:8.

[26] Matthew 10:16.

[27] Luke 6:36.

[28] KJV: *sporting themselves with their own deceivings*. Theophylact glosses this as "practiced in greed".

prophet. This is the logical sequence: "Spots they are and blemishes, well trained in avarice (that means, 'practiced in greed'), cursed children as they feast with you; having eyes full of adultery, and that cannot cease from sin, beguiling unstable souls." Paul called these "souls" *silly women laden with sins.*[29] These same men *have forsaken the right way, and followed the way of Balaam the son of Bosor etc.* Their words are *wells without water, clouds that are carried with a tempest etc.* And why is *the mist of darkness reserved* for them in the age to come? Because of their *great swelling words of vanity*, through which they *allure those who* used to *live in error* but were *clean escaped, through the lusts of the flesh, through much wantonness*, like *a dog turned to his own vomit again.* Everything in between is expounding and confirming the *vanity* of these men. This is the meaning: "They have nothing that remains pure, but are like spots on a clean garment with their tainted conduct. If they can manage to deceive some and make the men and women of their acquaintance ungodly, they count it pleasure, and so fill up the measure of their own ungodliness. And even when they feast with you it is not out of affection and a desire to break bread, but because they consider this an opportune time to beguile the women. For they have eyes that see nothing else other than adulteresses. And thus they cannot cease from looking and sinning, as cursed children, beguiling unstable souls. For their hearts are practiced at nothing other than avarice, that is 'ungodliness' and 'greed', and for these two things they have forsaken the right way, and are gone astray, following the way of Balaam son of Bosor." For he also *loved the wages of unrighteousness* and receiving bribes. *But he was rebuked for his iniquity: the dumb ass speaking with man's voice forbad the madness of the prophet.* This teaches us that after Balaam had been prevented once by God, he made haste to go to Balak a second time in his greed and arrogant passion, fueled by his frenzied sorcery. But constrained by the fear of God and the terrors of the journey, he did not counterfeit the message of the blessing. That message was not an act of "divination"; for those who understand what they utter are called "prophets". And thus he is called a *prophet*, since he understood what he was saying. After all, he would not have been able to choose the better option if he had not been aware of what he was saying. Therefore, the blessing is not an act of divination, but of the power of God.

---

[29] 2 Timothy 3:6.

2:17-19. These are wells without water, clouds that are carried with a tempest; to whom the mist of darkness is reserved for ever. For when they speak great swelling words of vanity, they allure through the lusts of the flesh, through much wantonness, those that were clean escaped from them who live in error. While they promise them liberty, they themselves are the servants of corruption: for of whom a man is overcome, of the same is he brought in bondage. Having given the lengthy example of Balaam, Peter now resumes his discussion of the immoral Gnostics that he had started at first. He portrays them as *wells without water*, for they have lost the pure message of the gospel and the water of life that it gives to drink. But he also compares them to *clouds* driven along by a contrary wind; he refers to this wind as a *tempest*, for it twists and distorts anything it drives before it. These are not bright clouds, like the saints, but full of *a mist of darkness*. He goes on to give the reason why: because *they speak great swelling words of vanity, they allure through the lusts of the flesh, through much wantonness, those that were clean escaped* once and for all, and had previously *lived in error*, but then entered the Lord's service. Moreover, he calls them *servants* of this same immorality, which he rightly calls *corruption*, even though *they promise liberty* to those who believe their deceit; thus, he introduces the paradoxical thought that they are *servants* of sin, even as they *promise liberty* to others. *For of whom a man is overcome, of the same is he brought in bondage.* This will be explained at length in the following passages.

2:20-22. For if after they have escaped the pollutions of the world through the knowledge of the Lord and Saviour Jesus Christ, they are again entangled therein, and overcome, the latter end is worse with them than the beginning. For it had been better for them not to have known the way of righteousness, than, after they have known it, to turn from the holy commandment delivered unto them. But it is happened unto them according to the true proverb, The dog is turned to his own vomit again; and the sow that was washed to her wallowing in the mire. By this point, Peter has established two things: that the one who is defeated is obliged to serve the one who defeats him, and that those who revert to their former ways after coming to the knowledge of the truth are worse off than they were before. Peter then illustrates these facts with a proverb. This is the general meaning: "So if these men have escaped the pollutions of the world through the knowledge of the Lord and Savior Jesus Christ, and are again entangled therein, and overcome, then they are obliged to serve those passions, and their bondage is worse than it was before they had gained the knowledge, for Satan will make certain that they come to a worse end. And so the Apostle says that if this is in store for those who take back the evils that they had renounced, it would be better for them to have never come to a knowledge of the truth, than having gained that knowledge to fall prey to worse evils. Just as when a dog is turned to his own vomit again, it is even more disgusting than it was before, and when a sow seeks again to wallow in the mire, her filth will appear all the filthier for it."

Chapter 3

3:1-2. This second epistle, beloved, I now write unto you; in both which I stir up your pure minds by way of remembrance: that ye may be mindful of the words which were spoken before by the holy prophets, and of the commandment of your apostles and of the Lord and Saviour.[30] From this we learn that there were two epistles of Peter in total. *In both which I stir up*, means, "in which epistles," or, "through which epistles *I stir up your pure minds*." For it takes a *pure mind* to be *mindful* of the salvation that it has already heard or committed to memory, and to be *stirred up* to bring it to mind with all its might and fervor (for it had already been committed to memory through the preaching of the *prophets* and the *apostles*.) In the same way Paul says: *And are built upon the foundation of the apostles and prophets.*[31] For all of these men proclaimed the coming of the Lord, and no one can disbelieve so many witnesses. "But why," says Peter, "do I mention the prophets and apostles? Because they proclaimed both the first and the second comings of our Lord and Savior." This is what he means by saying: *"Be mindful of the words which were spoken before by the holy prophets, by the commandment of your apostles, by the commandment of the Lord and Saviour."* The word *by* applies to both the *commandment of the apostles* and the *commandment of the Lord and Saviour*. Peter then goes on to tell them why he is urging them to call these things to mind: Those who live according to their passions and follow their own desires had noticed how some were apprehensive of the Lord's coming (which other men of God and even the Lord himself had foretold); this was leading them to reject their carefree lifestyle. So the evildoers attacked the believers and mocked them shamelessly, most of all because the event which the prophecy foretold had not immediately followed after it, but had been protracted in order to save those who are written of in the book of salvation.

3:3-5. Knowing this first, that there shall come in the last days scoffers, walking after their own lusts, and saying, Where is the promise of his coming? for since the fathers fell asleep, all things continue as they were

---

[30] KJV: *of us the apostles of the Lord and Savior.* Theophylact's text reads *your apostles*, which changes the whole meaning of the phrase.
[31] Ephesians 2:20.

from the beginning of the creation. For this they willingly are ignorant of: that by the word of God the heavens were of old, and the earth composed[32] of the water and in the water. According to Peter, the coming of the Lord did not occur immediately after it was foretold in order that many who are recorded in the book of the living might be saved. This is mocked by the *scoffers*, who attack the believers and say: *Where is the promise of his coming?* Just because one prophecy has not yet come to pass (for the reason that we have just given), is no reason for us to be taken aback by the opinions of evil men and disobey all the other commandments of the Lord that lead to salvation. Such was the mad policy of the Gnostics of that day, also known as Naassenes, Lampetians, and Euchites. Peter says they are all *willingly ignorant*, for they *willingly* shut their eyes to the truth. And what are they *ignorant* of? That according to Moses' account of creation, in the days of the flood, *the heavens* were made of *water* (for God commanded: *Let there be a firmament in the midst of the waters*),[33] and the earth likewise *appeared* out of the waters by his command, for it had been under the waters before. And just as the flood came unexpectedly over the heavens and the earth that *were composed of the water*, so now, the universe awaits destruction by fire, and the ungodly will likewise perish along with it. For there are only two elements that hold the universe together: water and fire. These are what give rise to the other two elements: "air" is clearly water that has evaporated, and "earth" is water that has been compacted. And no one in their right mind could fail to see that it is fire that both evaporates and compacts the water (for this is a natural property of fire that it is endowed with by the Creator God). So there are two elements, and if the former destruction of the ungodly happened by water, then according to Peter, the latter destruction must certainly happen by fire. *Of the water* describes the "material cause". *In the water* describes the "final cause". For it is water that holds the earth together, binding the dust of it tightly like glue, and giving it its form. If there were no water, then the earth would necessarily dissolve into dust and air. But someone might come after me with some nonsense like: "When God established the visible world, why did he not make it stable enough in the first place so that he would not need to go right back and restore it again, once by Noah's flood, and once by fire at the end of the

---

[32] KJV: *standing*. The text can mean "standing out of", "arising out of", "compacted out of". It can also mean "composed of", as Theophylact seems to understand it.
[33] Genesis 1:6.

age, as Peter is saying here?" Our reply: There was no way for the world to be free of entropy or change. How could it be, since it was by change that it had come into being in the first place? For it was made to exist out of non-existence—one would have to be a fool not to call that a "change"! And since entropy is nothing but a mixture of evil parts going from bad to worse, then the Creator will eventually have to restore it for the better, first cleansing it by water with Noah, and in the end, by fire. In the same way, we also refine materials in the fire, not in order to unmake them, but to render them pure and unadulterated. No one could fail to see this. Peter is saying that God has *promised* to do the same thing in the end. He will destroy the dross, and anything that does not directly contribute to human existence, such as plants, beasts, grass. All this dross will be perish to make way for life imperishable. If that is the case, then those who try to make this visible world out to have always been imperishable since the beginning must be out of their minds. And if anyone suspects that the same thing can be expected to happen to the intelligible substance, since it too was brought into being out of nothing, then he has not yet grasped that the simplicity of it makes it indestructible, as well as its proximity to the blessed substance and nature of God himself.

3:6. Through which[34] the world that then was, being overflowed with water, perished. *Through* the heavens and the earth; for the earth was overrun with water, while the skies poured down further cascades of water onto the land. Do not suppose that the entire world *perished*, but rather only the living creatures, which make the world what it is; for a world that is empty of them is not a world at all.

3:7. But the heavens and the earth, which are now, by the same word are kept in store, reserved unto fire against the day of judgment and perdition of ungodly men. Not only the Christians, but even the Greek scholars believe that the entire world will be destroyed by fire. Now someone will object: "What is the sense in establishing the world, if it is only bound for destruction?" We reply that the world is not bound for utter destruction, but rather renewal. Thus, the Prophet can say: *thou renewest the face of the earth.*[35] God first made visible creation to be "good", but because

---

[34] KJV: *Whereby.*

of mankind's transgression, creation itself *was made subject to vanity,*[36] that is, to unstable existence. Then came the flood, leaving but a few godly men on the earth, and as by a second renewal, the world began afresh through Noah, and the animals that were kept with him in the ark to raise up seed again in the world. But not even then did human nature keep its original condition, but rather degenerated and became worse than before; the law of Moses could not turn them from those evils, nor even the coming of the Lord. So while the call to salvation goes out in many forms, the destruction of disobedience is equally manifold; that is why the flood of fire must come. It is destruction, yes, but not utter destruction. Souls are not destroyed, nor even bodies. *For we must all appear before the judgment seat of Christ.*[37] Not in naked souls, stripped of our bodies, but with incorruptible bodies. For how could a soul stripped of its body be punished, and so *receive the things done in his body?*[38] For if two men have transgressed in the same way, no just judge would let one go, and lay on the other the full punishment for his crime. And besides, even we use fire to refine impure materials and reduce them to their essential state. *Reserved against the day of judgment and perdition*—the *against the day* refers equally to both, *against the day of judgment* and *against the day of perdition. Judgment* means "condemnation".

3:8-9. But, beloved, be not ignorant of this one thing, that one day is with the Lord as a thousand years, and a thousand years as one day. The Lord is not slack concerning his promise, as some men count slackness; but is longsuffering to us-ward, not willing that any should perish, but that all should come to repentance. Having finished his discourse on the end of the age with the conclusion that it must certainly come to pass, and must come by fire (all of which we have expounded at length), Peter now transitions to the protraction of the time until the end of the world, saying: "The Lord is not slack concerning his promise, as some men count slackness; but is longsuffering, for he awaits our salvation, and the full measure of those who are to be saved. For being himself eternal, nothing is protracted to him, but even a thousand years is as one day with

---

[35] Psalm 104:30.
[36] Romans 8:20.
[37] 2 Corinthians 5:10.
[38] 2 Corinthians 5:10.

him." Or rather not even the smallest fraction of a day, as David says when he compares *a thousand years* to *a watch in the night* (for he says: *a thousand years in thy sight are but as yesterday when it is past, and as a watch in the night.*[39] A *watch* represents the shortest unit of measurement). The night is divided into four segments, judging by how the Gospel says that the Lord *went unto* the holy apostles *[...] in the fourth watch of the night.*[40]

3:10-12. But the day of the Lord will come as a thief in the night; in the which the heavens shall pass away with a great noise, and the elements shall melt with fervent heat, the earth also and the works that are therein shall be burned up. Seeing then that all these things shall be dissolved, what manner of persons ought ye to be in all holy conversation and godliness, looking for and hasting unto the coming of the day of God, wherein the heavens being on fire shall be dissolved, and the elements shall melt with fervent heat? *Come as a thief in the night* refers to the mysterious and unexpected coming of the Lord: *in the night* describes the mystery of it, while *as a thief* describes the unexpected arrival. For no one would be robbed if they had already been expecting the thief. Thus, the Lord also says: *For as in the days that were before the flood they were eating and drinking,*[41] until the flood was at hand, *so shall also the coming of the Son of man be;*[42] it will come unexpectedly over the ungodly. *With a great noise* means "with a crackling"; for this is the telltale sound that objects make when they are consumed by fire. Note that he says, *the earth also and all the works that are therein shall be burned up,* but not the people (he only speaks of the *perdition of ungodly men,* that is, "destruction of their ungodly deeds"). For *the way of the ungodly shall perish,* but not the ungodly man himself.[43]

3:13-15a. Nevertheless we, according to his promise, look for new heavens and a new earth, wherein dwelleth righteousness. Wherefore, beloved, seeing that ye look for such things, be diligent that ye may be

---

[39] Psalm 90:4.
[40] Matthew 14:25.
[41] Matthew 24:38.
[42] Matthew 24:37.
[43] Psalm 1:6.

found of him in peace, without spot, and blameless. And account that the longsuffering of our Lord is salvation [...] The Lord will create *new heavens and a new earth*, but not out of new substance and material. Just as one who constructs a new house makes it out of preexisting materials, so God who once created matter and formed it into various shapes and combinations according to what suited his needs at the time, will dismiss whatever is unprofitable and extraneous for the imperishable things to come. Whatever is profitable, however, he will reform with imperishable and indescribable beauty and give it a place in the second, imperishable world.

3:15b-18. [...] even as our beloved brother Paul also according to the wisdom given unto him hath written unto you; as also in all his epistles, speaking in them of these things; in which are some things hard to be understood, which they that are unlearned and unstable wrest, as they do also the other scriptures, unto their own destruction. Ye therefore, beloved, seeing ye know these things before, beware lest ye also, being led away with the error of the wicked, fall from your own stedfastness. But grow in grace, and in the knowledge of our Lord and Saviour Jesus Christ. To him be glory both now and for ever. Amen. Paul had said this as well: *not knowing that the goodness of God leadeth thee to repentance?*[44] So if the *longsuffering* of God *leadeth us to repentance*, then *repentance* brings us deliverance. Thus, the *longsuffering* of God is for our benefit and salvation. *Hard to understand* refers to the things that are proclaimed in a distorted fashion even among the ungodly. That is what *wrest* means. To give one telling illustration, Saint Paul says this: *Moreover the law entered, that the offence might abound. But where sin abounded, grace did much more abound.*[45] But they distort it, making Paul out to say: "Let us sin more, that we may be forgiven more." This they do *unto their own destruction*. For those who kill the words of the prophets and the apostles by distorting them incur the same judgment as the very ones that killed them. For they killed them in order to stop their disciples from profiting from the doctrine of salvation, lest any of them lay hold of salvation. Peter refers to faith in the Lord as one's own *stedfastness*. And just as he concludes his other epistle

---

[44] Romans 2:4.
[45] Romans 5:20.

with a prayer, so also in this one he wishes them to grow in the faith of the Lord.

The end of the Second Epistle of the holy Apostle Peter; 154 verses.

The Explanation of Jude

Summary

Jude writes this letter to those who have already come to faith. This is the occasion: *Certain men had crept in unawares* and were *denying Christ*, teaching that sin is of no consequence. *It was needful* for him to write and reassure the brothers. He first enjoins them to *contend for* and abide in *the faith which was once delivered*. He then pronounces such men deceivers and instructs that no one should have fellowship with them, for they know that it is not sufficient to be merely called, yet not walk worthily of the calling. For the Lord led the people of old out of Egypt, and destroyed those who did not abide in the faith. Likewise he did not spare, *the angels which kept not their own estate*. Thus, we must withdraw from such men. For even Michael the archangel would not suffer the slander of the devil. But as he teaches, their destruction will be as that of Sodom. Next, he gives instruction concerning morality. And having prayed for the Lord to grant them stability in the faith, he concludes the epistle.[46]

---

[46] All Scripture references and versification follow the King James Version (KJV), except where the original wording is of particular relevance to Theophylact's argument. In such cases, the Greek is rendered more directly and the KJV text is given in a footnote.

Major Themes

i. *On attention to faith in Christ because of the resistance of ungodly and lascivious men*

ii. *On their impending punishment after the likeness of the sinners and evildoers of old*

iii. *Assessment of their wretched estate: deceit, ungodliness, lasciviousness, blasphemy, false hypocrisy, and bribery for the sake of deception*

iv. *On security for them in the faith, compassion and mercy toward their neighbor, for their holiness and salvation*

v. *A prayer for their holiness and pure confidence, together with praise for God*

Chapter 1

1a. Jude, the servant of Jesus Christ, and brother of James, to them that are sanctified by God the Father [...] It was glory enough for him, (for the present apostle I mean), after calling himself a *servant of Christ*, to associate himself with the honorable James. For since the virtue of James was extolled by all, it rendered him more suitable to his hearers to teach the word, since after all, he who shares in birth and blood would not seem wholly estranged in manners as well from his kinsman. And he likewise states that he and his brother alike pull the same yoke of *servitude* to the same *Christ*.

1b-2. [...] and preserved in Jesus Christ, and called: Mercy unto you, and peace, and love, be multiplied. Here this blessed man shows that the word of the Lord was true when he said, *no man can come to me, except the Father which hath sent me draw him.*[47] For he says that those who are loved by the Father are *preserved in Jesus Christ*. That is why he also says they are *called*. For this is not of their own design, but by the Father, because he is the one who *drew* them and *called* them. He wishes for *mercy, peace, and love to be multiplied* unto them. *Mercy*, because it was by his *tender mercy* that we were called up to him and received as his servants; *peace*, because God the Father himself has granted us this as well, through his Son Jesus Christ, who has reconciled us even though we had offended him; and *love*, because it was for the sake of his love for us that his only begotten Son was given over to death on our behalf. Jude prays that these things be bestowed on them ever more abundantly, joining his voice with the blessed David: *O continue thy mercy*[48] *unto them that know thee*. So let us also, inspired by these examples of salvation, show unfeigned love to the brothers and live in a manner worthy of him who *called* us.

3a. Beloved, when I gave all diligence to write unto you of the common salvation, it was needful for me to write unto you [...] Here Jude lays out the subject of the letter, namely to ensure their salvation, lest in their simplicity they be captured by the abominable heretics; hence he writes these words as if to brand them and make them apparent to those who are

---

[47] John 6:44.
[48] KJV: *lovingkindness*.

not aware, by exposing their immoral lifestyle. Peter had likewise spoken concerning them, but Jude writes more clearly here. He says that they were *written of before of old*, since both Peter and Paul had spoken about how such deceivers would come in the last days. Even Christ himself had spoken of them: *For many shall come in my name [...] and shall deceive many [...] go ye not therefore after them.*[49] For by calling themselves "Christians", they will lead many astray by that *name*. This is referring to the followers of the abominable Nicolas, Valentine, and Simon. These men were wanton gluttons and only made a pretense of this teaching, that they might find and, *lead captive silly women laden with sins.*[50] They concocted certain nightly rituals and gave themselves over to *chambering and wantonness.*[51] The phrase, *turning [...] into lasciviousness*, means, "converting, counterfeiting from temperance into immorality". That is why our Lord Jesus Christ rejects them. And how could they not be rejected who drove away the teacher of all temperance by their unclean lives, as if by cries and shrieks? *For what fellowship hath righteousness with unrighteousness?*[52]

3b-4. [...] and exhort you that ye should earnestly contend for the faith which was once delivered unto the saints. For there are certain men crept in unawares, who were before of old ordained to this condemnation, ungodly men, turning the grace of our God into lasciviousness, and denying our only Master, God, and Lord Jesus Christ.[53] Jude *exhorts* those who have *once* accepted our Lord and Savior Jesus Christ and believed on him to *earnestly contend*. For if we have accepted the incarnation of the Word, yet still profess that the pre-eternal Word of the Father and the son of his mother were two different and distinct persons, how could we not be *denying* our one *Lord and Master*? For the Lord Jesus is One according to the economy of his union. The pre-eternal Word of God and God himself, possesses flesh which is exalted to the glory of his divinity, which he received by his conception from the holy Virgin in the beginning, and is one and the same *Master* of all.

---

[49] See Mark 13:6, Luke 21:8.
[50] 2 Timothy 3:6.
[51] Romans 13:13.
[52] 2 Corinthians 6:14.
[53] KJV: *the only Lord God, and our Lord Jesus Christ.* The KJV takes this as a reference to God the Father and Jesus Christ, while Theophylact sees only a single reference to Christ.

5-7. I will therefore put you in remembrance, though ye once knew this, how that the Lord, having saved the people out of the land of Egypt, afterward destroyed them that believed not. And the angels which kept not their first estate, but left their own habitation, he hath reserved in everlasting chains under darkness unto the judgment of the great day. Even as Sodom and Gomorrha, and the cities about them in like manner, giving themselves over to fornication, and going after strange flesh, are set forth for an example, suffering the vengeance of eternal fire. Having now spoken of the wantonness of the vile Nicolaitans, Valentinians, and Marcionites, Jude goes on: *the Lord, having saved the people out of the land of Egypt, etc.* He thereby proves that he is both the God of the Old Testament and the Inaugurator of the New, but not as those abominable men claim, that the God of the Old Testament is vindictive and cruel, while the God of the New Testament is gentle and loving toward mankind. And just as Jude's current generation will not remain unpunished, neither did the generation of Egypt. And although God delivered them from the violence of Egypt in order to display his overwhelming might and because of the oath he had sworn to their fathers, nevertheless they did not remain unpunished when they transgressed, but paid the penalty they deserved; and both the favor God had shown to their fathers and the miracles wrought by such supernatural operation availed them not. Those who had passed through the Red Sea on dry land, and later fell away from the faith, perished. Those, moreover, who had been allotted the honor of angelic rank, and through carelessness did not retain their *estate*, but neglected the heavenly polity granted them out of kindness, he has *reserved* unto *judgment*, meaning "the sentence of punishment" on the great day (for that is the significance of *reserved*). Or as the Lord also says, *everlasting fire, prepared for the devil and his angels*.[54] In the same way, the Sodomites *set forth an example* of the *everlasting fire* that will engulf them. *Going after strange flesh*, likewise refers to "fornicating" or "turning aside", which is fornication. *Strange flesh* denotes the "male nature", for it cannot lead to childbirth through intimate relations. It is rather the "female" whose *flesh* is for intimate relations, just as our forefather said: *Bone of my bones, and flesh of my flesh*.[55] The *flesh* of males is *strange*, in the sense of "unfit for

---

[54] Matthew 25:45.
[55] Genesis 2:23.

intimate relations". But as for females, as the laws stipulate, one woman for one man, his very own flesh. While the *flesh* of a loose woman and a harlot is *strange* and foreign, and only slightly less of an abomination than that of the male.

8. Likewise also these filthy dreamers defile the flesh, despise dominion, and speak evil of glories.[56] Having given all these examples leading up to this point, Jude leaves the conclusion to his hearer's imagination. And what is that? It is this: "If therefore he treated them this way, with no inhibitions because of their former blessed estate, then will he really make an exception for those who are now sinning, because the Son of God entered into the world on account of mankind, and suffered their scorn, and was tested by suffering? Let none say this! For although he loves mankind, he is yet just in his faithfulness. And indeed it is because of the faithfulness of his justice that he did not spare those who had sinned. While at the same time because of his love for mankind, he welcomed harlots and tax collectors into the kingdom." This is the wonted conclusion, which Jude omits, either because of the reason we have already stated, or because the blessed Peter had already anticipated him when he said, *if God spared not the angels that sinned, etc.*[57] But enough about that. The phrase, *filthy dreamers defile the flesh*, is put remarkably delicately. The word *dreamers* is a euphemism for the extreme vileness of the action. We shall disclose some of what he has omitted, which we have learned from the work of the blessed Epiphanius of Cyprus, which he entitled *The Panarion*. He says that these people were known as the Borborites, and would have sordid and abominable relations with women in which they would not release their seed into the womb, but before the abominable act was complete, they would take it in their own hands and immediately put it in the mouths of the women they were consorting with, and thus these vile men would leave proud of what they had accomplished. This impure action was known as a *dream*, because it was done before the act was complete. So that is the kind of *dreams* they were having. After *defiling their own flesh* by this obscene offering, he says, they go on to rage[58] against the divine nature, *despising* his *dominion* and his lordship over everything. The blessed Irenaeus, Bishop of Lyons, goes into

---

[56] KJV: *dignitaries*. See the many interpretations of this word below.
[57] 2 Peter 2:4.
[58] In Greek, there is a play on the words *miainō* ("defile") and *mainomai* ("rage").

more depth concerning them in his work entitled, *Refutation of the So-Called Knowledge. Otherwise*. He denounces their impiety, saying that both their lifestyle is impure and their knowledge is irreverent. He accuses them of *despising dominion*, meaning the ceremony of the mystery of Christ. For they *despise* it by perpetrating their impious acts instead of the angelic mysteries. *Speaking evil of glories*. The *glories* or "opinions"[59] should be taken as the many ideas of trustworthy men, which the foremost of the Greeks call "propositions", and define them as innovative ideas, not of common men, but of those learned in philosophy. For Moses also appeared to have radical ideas, when he tried to introduce strange customs to the members of the community, and likewise the holy apostles with the changes God inspired them to make in people's lives. And so those people were not slow to refer to their ideas as *opinions*. The godly Paul further confirms this, for when he was taken up to Mars Hill by the Athenians and there discussed with them the things of God, they also considered him a *babbler* by the time he finished.[60] And just as they mocked what he said as *babbling*, so also they called these things *opinions*. And so this holy man used the term *opinions* because it was common and well-known to all, referring to men gifted by God. *Or yet otherwise. Glories*, refers to the Old and New Testaments, as Paul says: *For if that which is done away was by glory,[61] much more that which remaineth is in glory.[62]* Or else, *glories* refers to the ecclesiastical authorities that they were slandering. Likewise, we can ascertain from the third epistle of the beloved John, where he says that Diotrephes was, *prating against us with malicious words.[63]* By mentioning, *speaking evil*, he calls not only them, but all men to reason, and to keep their tongues clear of such evil, and not even to *speak evil* of those who deserve it: *Yet Michael the archangel, etc*. What does this mean? He means that these men *speak evil* freely and without restraint against anyone. But this is not as it should be, for it is not even right to *speak evil* of those who deserve to be *spoken evil* of. This is clear from the example of Michael the archangel. For while he could have *spoken evil* of the devil for his insolence when he was, *contending with the devil about the body of Moses*, he did not

---

[59] The word *doxa* "glory" can also refer to someone's "opinion".
[60] Acts 17:18.
[61] KJV: *glorious*.
[62] 2 Corinthians 3:11. KJV: *glorious*.
[63] 3 John 10.

do this, but merely replied with, "the Lord alone rebuke thee, devil." If this is how the archangel behaved, then we also should not bring *accusations* against our fellow men and brothers in court.[64] For this is the meaning of the contest *about the body of Moses*: It is said in the apocrypha that Michael the archangel officiated at the burial of Moses. The devil, however, did not accept this, but brought accusations against him because he murdered the Egyptian,[65] and insisted that Moses was guilty on this account, and would not allow him to receive funerary honors. The apostle now mentions this not only to teach us not to be quick to *bring accusations*, but also to show that all men will be obliged to come forth and settle accounts once they have been parted from the body, and that the God of the New Testament is the same as the God of the Old; and that after we have left this world, the devil will oppose our souls with his evil demons, in order to hinder their safe passage. Yes, he will rise up in opposition, but the good angels will fight on behalf of our souls, as in the vision of the blessed Anthony. In the end, the devil yielded. However, Jude says that Michael did not denounce the devil at that time, and did not rebuke him with authority, but instead yielded the judgment to the Lord of all, saying: *the Lord rebuke thee*, devil.

9-11. Yet Michael the archangel, when contending with the devil he disputed about the body of Moses, durst not bring against him a railing accusation, but said, The Lord rebuke thee. But these speak evil of those things which they know not: but what they know naturally, as brute beasts, in those things they corrupt themselves. Woe unto them! for they have gone in the way of Cain, and ran greedily after the error of Balaam for reward, and perished in the gainsaying of Core. Jude says, "Michael would not even suffer the devil to *bring a railing accusation* against a man, that is, Moses. But these men concoct slanderous speeches against doctrines *of which they know not. But what they know* by instinct of *nature, as brute beasts*, these things they pursue, *as fed horses in the morning: every one neighed after his neighbour's wife.*[66] *Woe unto them! For they have gone in the way of Cain*, who slew his brother, for they likewise have taught such things to their brothers, their own flesh and blood, and slain them by their wicked doctrine. Or else that by consuming their

---

[64] The word *blasphēmia* can mean "accusation" or "slander" as well as "speaking evil".
[65] See Exodus 2:12.
[66] Jeremiah 5:8.

own seed, they slay those who could potentially have been their brothers, whose seed could have blossomed into life. *The error of Balaam*, means that they too, like him, do these things *for reward*, while *the gainsaying of Core* means that they too, like him, were undeserving of the rank of teacher, but yet they laid hold of it nonetheless.

12a. These are reefs[67] in your feasts of charity, when they feast with you [...] At that time, there were still communal meals being held in the churches, as Paul mentions in Corinthians. These were known as *feasts of charity*.[68] Jude continues: "They gather for these, not to fulfill their rightful purpose, but that they might find occasion to *beguile unstable souls*,[69] as Peter also says in his second epistle. Jude compares them to *reefs, clouds without water, trees whose fruit withereth,* and *wandering stars*; what such things possess by nature, these men possess by choice. For *reefs* are the bane of those who sail, and catch them unawares, just as these men inflict evil on their unsuspecting fellows at the *feast*. In the same way, *clouds without water, carried about of winds*, do not refresh the regions where they are borne with rain (for they have none), but only plunge them into darkness. Thus, these men do not yield the rain of salvation onto the souls of those who listen to them, but only darken them with their abominable expositions, *carried about* into the evil enterprises of the demons. Likewise, *trees whose fruit withereth, twice dead*, once when their leaves fall off (for then they are seen to be dry, robbed of their splendor, the glory of their fruit, and the majesty of their verdant boughs), and these men suffer a similar fate. And *twice dead*, by eating their own seed, and distancing themselves from prudent and well-ordered society. Thus they are *plucked up by the roots* and cast out of the garden of the Lord's church, gathered up and thrown out into the eternal fire. For what kind of *roots* could such men have, who are abhorred by all for their abominable lifestyle? They are also called *wandering stars*, not because they adorn the firmament of our faith, through which Christ, the Sun, travels, and appoints the hours of virtues, giving life to the faithful through them, but rather because they can appear to change their shape into an angel of light, just as their evil demonic leader, and do nothing but oppose the teachings of the Lord. They darken those who come

---

[67] KJV: *spots*. The meaning of this word is uncertain, see 2 Peter 2:13.

[68] Greek *agapē*.

[69] 2 Peter 2:14.

to them, and yield eternal darkness for themselves. But they are also compared to *raging waves*, and the likeness is undeniable. For they too are *carried about* without reason or restraint by the evil blasphemies of spirits,[70] *foaming out their own shame*, ending only in foam, like the blasphemous world, because of the shamefulness of their unstable and fleeting lives. Such men are those whom Jude compares to the foam of the waves.

12b-13. [...] feeding themselves without fear: clouds they are without water, carried about of winds; trees whose fruit withereth, without fruit, twice dead, plucked up by the roots; Raging waves of the sea, foaming out their own shame; wandering stars, to whom is reserved the blackness of darkness for ever. The *without fear* either refers to the *reefs*, in which case the meaning would be this: "reefs feasting with you without fear", meaning "bringing destruction on the unsuspecting souls of those who feast with them, like reefs". Or, *without fear* should go with *feeding themselves*, yielding the following meaning: "feeding themselves without fear", not worried that shepherds who do not know how to feed their sheep will be judged, *blind leaders of the blind*, and as the Lord said, they and their sheep will *fall into a ditch*.[71]

14-18. And Enoch also, the seventh from Adam, prophesied of these, saying, Behold, the Lord cometh with ten thousands of his saints, to execute judgment upon all, and to convince all that are ungodly among them of all their ungodly deeds which they have ungodly committed, and of all their hard speeches which ungodly sinners have spoken against him. These are murmurers, complainers, walking after their own lusts; and their mouth speaketh great swelling words, having men's persons in admiration because of advantage. But, beloved, remember ye the words which were spoken before of the apostles of our Lord Jesus Christ; How that they told you there should be mockers in the last time, who should walk after their own ungodly lusts. Having said all these things, Jude now mentions Enoch, who prophesied of the punishment that was stored up for them by God in the last days; that is, the righteous *judgment* of the Lord. The *ungodly* man is different than the *sinner*. For

---

[70] In Greek, *pneuma* can mean "spirit" or "wind".
[71] Matthew 15:14.

ungodly errs in relation to God, while the *sinner* errs in what he does in life, missing the mark of righteousness. Then, forsaking the example of the *ungodly*, Jude transitions directly to his indictment of them, calling them *murmurers* and *complainers* against what is good. A *murmurer* is one who grumbles under his breath and in secret against something he finds distasteful; a *complainer* is one who is always mocking everything. Jude says that these men are *murmurers* and *complainers*. "For their doctrine is too shameful to teach in public. For it is quite perilous to broadcast their ungodliness, with its immorality and blasphemy. They are *complainers*, because they speak ill of the teaching of others and the truth in order to establish their own evils and abominations." As was said of Balaam as well, these men also, *run greedily for reward.* Now Jude says more clearly that they, *have men's persons in admiration because of advantage.* To "have someone in admiration" means to treat those in power with flattery. "Advantage" means "profit".

19. These be they who separate,[72] natural,[73] having not the Spirit. Here now is another charge laid against these abominable men. "For," says Jude, "they are not the only ones who perish, but they also rob the Church of her children (for that is what *separate* means)." That is, "they remove them from the bounds of the church", or "from the faith", or "from the very tabernacle of the church". For having proved that their own assemblies are dens of thieves, they draw others away from the Church, and to themselves. They do this because they are *natural* people, meaning, "living according to the behavior of the world". For, as we have already said, the holy Scriptures often refer to "life" as the "soul".[74] Such as in Job: *All that a man hath will he give for his soul,*[75] that is, "for his life". Paul likewise says that, *the natural man receiveth not the things of the Spirit of God.*[76] Since therefore they are *natural*, their teaching is likewise *natural*, of which it is said: *This wisdom descendeth not from above, but is earthly, natural,[77] devilish,* and does not have the voice of the Spirit of God.

---

[72] KJV: *separate themselves.*

[73] KJV: *sensual.*

[74] In Greek, the word translated as "natural", *psychikos*, is derived from the word *psychē* "soul" or "life".

[75] Job 2:4, KJV: *life.*

[76] 1 Corinthians 2:14.

[77] KJV: *sensual.*

20-23a. But ye, beloved, building up yourselves on your most holy faith, praying in the Holy Ghost, keep yourselves in the love of God, looking for the mercy of our Lord Jesus Christ unto eternal life. And of some have compassion who make a difference:[78] And others save with fear, pulling them out of the fire [...] "The natural men," says Jude, "are as we have described them. But you, building yourselves up in the Holy Spirit and the most holy faith, that is, reestablishing yourselves in the Holy Spirit, which means, by the teaching of the Holy Spirit, convening your assemblies in your prayers, keep yourselves in the love of God; that is, guard yourselves, receiving the mercy that comes from the Lord, which is unto eternal life and will be awarded to you on the last day. But if they separate from you (for this is what "making a difference" means), refute them, that is, reveal their immorality to all. However, if they seek reconciliation, do not reject them, but accept them by the mercy of your love, saving them out of the impending fire. But receive them with mercy and with fear, and take care lest you be unmindful of them and this acceptance should be a cause of corruption among you; and thus you who are already firmly grounded should be plunged unawares into the same chaos of immorality that they are in. For evil is seductive. So when you receive them, you should take them in with fear, that is, with caution, and let the mercy you show them be accompanied by hatred of their vile deeds. Hate and despise even the smallest garment stained by their flesh, for even contact with their flesh is called "hateful". Or receive them in fear of the coming punishment, and render them worthy of mercy by repentance."

23b. [...] hating even the garment spotted by the flesh. Now unto him that is able to keep you from falling, and to present you faultless before the presence of his glory with exceeding joy, To the only wise God our Saviour, be glory and majesty, dominion and power, both now and ever. Amen. The *garment* is *spotted* with the many sins from the life of the flesh wallowing in the passions. For everyone is seen by his conduct in life, as by a kind of garment, whether he be righteous or unrighteous. He whose *garment* is pure has a virtuous life, while he whose *garment* is *spotted* has a life of evil deeds. Or rather the *garment* is *spotted by the flesh*, whose habits

---

[78] KJV: *making a difference*.

and dispositions give shape to the soul, through the conscience, by the memory of the evil motions and actions perpetrated in the flesh. The soul beholds these things at all times, as a *garment* wrapped around it, and is filled with the stench of the passions. Just as the soul can also be clothed in the *garment* of incorruptibility, woven together of virtues by the Spirit, which it wears and becomes beautiful and glorious, so also can it be clothed in a filthy and *spotted garment*, woven similarly together out of passions of the flesh. And this is how the soul is then seen, having taken on another form and image, other than that of God. And having said these things, Jude seals his epistle with a prayer.

End of the Epistle of the holy Apostle Jude, 68 verses.

Printed in Great Britain
by Amazon

18752197R00031